First World War
and Army of Occupation
War Diary
France, Belgium and Germany

34 DIVISION
Divisional Troops
'E' Squadron North Irish Horse
11 January 1916 - 29 April 1916

WO95/2445/1

The Naval & Military Press Ltd
www.nmarchive.com
Published in association with The National Archives

Published by

The Naval & Military Press Ltd

Unit 10 Ridgewood Industrial Park,

Uckfield, East Sussex,

TN22 5QE England

Tel: +44 (0) 1825 749494

www.naval-military-press.com

www.nmarchive.com

This diary has been reprinted in facsimile from the original. Any imperfections are inevitably reproduced and the quality may fall short of modern type and cartographic standards.

© Crown Copyright
Images reproduced by permission of The National Archives, London, England, 2015.

Contents

Document type	Place/Title	Date From	Date To
Miscellaneous	WO95/2445/1		
Miscellaneous	E Sqdn Nth Irish Horse		
Heading	34th Division Divl Troops "E" Sqdn Nth Irish Horse Jan-Apr 1916		
Heading	E Squadron N. Irish Horse Vol 1		
War Diary	Longbridge Deverill	11/01/1916	11/01/1916
War Diary	Havre	12/01/1916	12/01/1916
War Diary	Blendecques	12/01/1916	12/01/1916
War Diary	Ebblinghem	20/01/1916	23/01/1916
War Diary	Estaires	24/01/1916	31/01/1916
Miscellaneous	E. Sq. North. Irish Horse Vol 2		
War Diary	Estaires	01/02/1916	18/02/1916
War Diary	Steenwerck	19/02/1916	29/02/1916
Miscellaneous	E N I Horse Vol 3		
War Diary	Steenwerck	03/03/1916	10/03/1916
War Diary	Croix Du Bac	17/03/1916	11/04/1916
War Diary	Sec Bois	12/04/1916	12/04/1916
War Diary	Scaderbourg	15/04/1916	19/04/1916
War Diary	Journy	20/04/1916	29/04/1916

WO69/2445/1

E SQDN NTH IRISH HORSE

34TH DIVISION
DIVL TROOPS

'E' SQDN NTH IRISH HORSE.
JAN - APR 1916

To 7 Corps

"E" Squadron N. in'h Horse
Vol: I
Jan '16

3rd Div.

WAR DIARY
or
INTELLIGENCE SUMMARY

Army Form C. 2118

(Erase heading not required.) North Irish Horse (34th Inf Div)

Place	Date	Hour	Summary of Events and Information	Remarks and references to Appendices
LONGBRIDGE DEVERILL	11/1/16	11 am	Left camp to entrain at COTFORD for France. Horse waggons loaded in 10 min. Arrived S'hampton Docks 6pm. On board S.S. Rossetti & Newport Mort dame by 7.20. Sailed 8 pm.	
HAVRE	12/1/16		Arrived off the harbour early in morning. Entered docks midday. Disembarked by 1.20 pm. Sqdn Hqr billeted & Sqd Hqrs direct mobilisation stores which could not be issued before leaving England. Entrained at 5pm at No.4 Pr. Entraining arrangements compared most unfavourably with those at COTFORD. Forms fatigue parties were demanded by the RTO which had was impracticable. Method for entraining in France suggested as follows:- (1) Each troop to load at same time. (2) About each troop 5 trucks 4 of which for horses & the 5th for equipment to form 4 horse 1 equipment truck a portable gangway to load 6 horses & 2 men on each. Saddlery to be in truck the horse & 2 men so march. Horses were fed again at 7pm and watered & fed at 6.20 am at ABBEVILLE.	
BLENDECQUES	12/1/16	3pm	Arrived. Ishaved most satisfaction in considering the great loss of confusion that the method of entrainment has put the Sqdn in at HAVRE. Received orders to proceed to	

Army Form C. 2118

WAR DIARY
or
INTELLIGENCE SUMMARY

(Erase heading not required.)

North Irish Horse (34th Inf. Div.)

Place	Date	Hour	Summary of Events and Information	Remarks and references to Appendices
EBBLINGHEM	20/1/16		EBBLINGHEM (6½ miles distant) and billet settled mainly - 2 Tp J.H. Gregg & 1st interpreter were sent on in advance - Arrived in billets at 6= ESBLINGHEM at 6.20 p.m.	
"	22/1/16	10 pm	O.C. 34th Inf. inspected the styles in billets	
"	23/1/16		Received instructions to proceed to ESTAIRES. (21 miles distant) 7.55 am marched. Halted for 15 min about 12.30 pm to water & give horses a small feed. Horses behaved remarkably Stop 10 min. a 2.0. Walked with horses in hand about 4½ miles - Arrived ESTAIRES 3.15 Quickly got into billets -	
ESTAIRES	24/1/16		General clean up of horse lines billets just vacated by Cumberland Yeo.	
	25 to 31st /16		Nothing of particular interest -	

J.W. [signature]
Comm. [Cav.]
34th Inf. Cav.

E Sy. Worth
Irish Horse
Vol 2
34

Army Form C. 2118

WAR DIARY
or
INTELLIGENCE SUMMARY
(Erase heading not required.) E Sqdn No1K Ind Horse — 34 K Ind Cav

Instructions regarding War Diaries and Intelligence Summaries are contained in F. S. Regs., Part II. and the Staff Manual respectively. Title Pages will be prepared in manuscript.

Place	Date	Hour	Summary of Events and Information	Remarks and references to Appendices
ESTAIRES	Feby 16th		On January 29th, 12 N.C.O's & men and on the 10th Feby 20 N.C.O's & men went for a Course of Road Control under A.P.M. 34th Div at BLAIRINGHEM. The first party rejoined at ESTAIRES on Feby 3rd. The second party rejoined at Steenwerck on Feby 18th.	
Do	Feby 16th		2nd Lt Doneiji & 12 NCOs & men left for course of "Sniping"	
Do	Feby 17th		1 Sergt & 10 men sent to guard Bridge at BAC ST MAUR. They were relieved on 20th.	
Do	18th		The Squadron left ESTAIRES 8.15am arrived STEENWERCK 9.45am. Good turn out & nothing left behind	
STEENWERCK	19th	8.7pm	Received orders either in billets or stables. "Turn out" Squadron including 1st line Transport was on Road ready to move anywhere at 8.37pm. At 9.30pm received orders to "dismiss". All 2nd line Transport was ready to take in it required. 1 Sergt & 4 men were detailed as Guard with lantern orders were received and to load baggage wagon & supply wagon it required.	
Do	Feby 20		Supplied 2 Sergts & 22 men for duty under A.P.M. 34 K Div. Took over guard) at BAC ST MAUR BR. 1 Sergt and 11 men	

WAR DIARY or INTELLIGENCE SUMMARY

Army Form C. 2118

(2)

Place	Date	Hour	Summary of Events and Information	Remarks and references to Appendices
Neuve Eglise	21st		Supplied 45 men for fatigue at BRICKWORKS SAILLY. This left the Squadron with 2 available men to water & feed 143 horses at midday	
"	20th		Sent 1 Officer & 20 men to take over "Salvage" of 23rd Div at ERQUINGHEM permanently	
"	22nd		Supplied 15 men for fatigue at SAILLY	
"	23rd		Do. Do. The Squadron from a Military point of view as an "effective unit" now practically ceased to exist. 23 NCOs & men & 3 officers could be put into the firing line in a sudden emergency	
"	24th		Fatigue 25 men	
"	25th		Do.	
"	26th		do	
"	27th		No fatigue!	
"	28th		1 Cpl & 6 men detailed for guard over RE Dump at ARMENTIERES	
"	29th		Have 19 men I could put into action myself all including trackless	

JA Hulburn Capt
Comdg Sqn
30th Jun 1915

"Ē" N I Hare

Vol 3

3⁴

WAR DIARY
or
INTELLIGENCE SUMMARY

Army Form C.2118

E Sqdn North Irish Horse
34th (K) III Corps Cav-

(Erase heading not required.)

Instructions regarding War Diaries and Intelligence Summaries are contained in F.S. Regs., Part II. and the Staff Manual respectively. Title Pages will be prepared in manuscript.

Place	Date	Hour	Summary of Events and Information	Remarks and references to Appendices
STEENWERCK	3/3/16		1 Officer & 28 men detailed for permanent duty under A.P.M.	"Particularly no enemy activity on our front. Stables with hurdle roofs, shelter fences etc during our stay. Horses inlines"
"	"	9.15	2 NCOs & 6 men detailed for road control at L'ETANETTE	
"	"	10.15	2 Lt G.H. Grigg & 2 OR left for III Corps School of Sniping	
"	17/3		Changed billets -	
"	18/3		1 Cpl & men left for School of Instruction in Hotchkiss gun.	
"	20/3		The following letter was received of this date "for circulation amongst the instructors with state and summary of your sqdn" – (signed) A.H. 19.49	Changed bilts at Greatly to heart 6.5m comparée -
CROIX DU BAC	22nd 23rd		"K.IV." - Advance guard to a divn. was practised with all available men - 2 men left for III Corps Sniping School -	
"	25th		2 Lt G.H. Grigg went to Hinckles with 5 ORs - "Sniping"	
"	28th		3 men & 6 horses sent to 7th Sqdn R.F.C. to use of Mons.	
"	31st		2 Lt N.F. Turling left to join 2 Lt G.H. Grigg "Sniping" with 2 Lt R.B. Killock & men left for LA BOUDRELLE school of instruction -	
"	do		STATE of Sqdn as at 31st:-	

Bridge Guard 18 OR (dismounted)
A.P.M. Salvage 10 + 28 OR
School of Instruction 10, 3 OR
"Hot. Snipers" 2, 0, 10 OR
1 Man hospital
1 on Special leave - R.F. Corps -
Total with Sqdn. 2.0. 75 OR 106 horses
34 (K) III Corps Cav-

Capt
Commdg
E Sqdn North Irish Horse

WAR DIARY or INTELLIGENCE SUMMARY

Army Form C. 2118

(E Sqdrn) E IV (4)
Vol 4

Place	Date	Hour	Summary of Events and Information	Remarks and references to Appendices
CROIX DU BAC	April 1-6		Established for duty under ATM. 1 Officer 28 OR. "Sniping" 2 Officers 8 OR. "Bridge Guards 16. OR.	
do		7.10	"Sqdn Drill, minor schemes etc "Snipers" with drums from hinder.	
do		10.15	Bridge guards withdrawn -	
do		11.15	APM troops withdrawn & Sqdn paraded 2pm proceeded to SEC BOIS arriving 5pm.	
SEC BOIS	12th	8am	Proceeded to billets at SCADERBOURG (ST MARTIN) arriving 4pm.	
SCADER-BOURG	13-18-		Provisional training programme of 34th Div. commenced which included sword & rifle drill, musketry & range practice. Physical drill. Riding up drill. Reports - scouting, vetting. Study of ground map reading. Resting & sport return relay system at truth.	
	20/15 19/15		Paraded 8am proceeded to JOURNY the attached 2nd Can Div. - Arrives in billets 12 noon.	
JOURNY	20-29/15		Training in duties of Mt Mounted Troops under Capt Wickham 15th Hussars in conjunction with 24th Div Cyclist Coy -	

J A Hinley Capt
E Sqdrn Cdt

www.ingramcontent.com/pod-product-compliance
Lightning Source LLC
Chambersburg PA
CBHW081254170426
43191CB00037B/2153